arranged by Alan Gout

Classic
Jazz Standards
for B♭ clarinet
& piano

Klassische Jazz *standards*
für Klarinette in B
und Klavier

Classics du jazz
pour clarinette en si bémol
et piano

Contents

FABER *ff* MUSIC

© 1995 by Faber Music Ltd
First published in 1995 by Faber Music Ltd
3 Queen Square, London WC1N 3AU
Cover design by S & M Tucker
Music processed by Chris Hinkins
Printed in England by Halstan & Co Ltd

ISBN 0 571 51558 4

1. Tin Roof Blues

George Brunies, Ben Pollack, Paul Mares,
Leon Rappolo & Mel Stitzel.
Lyrics by Walter Melrose.

* Small notes ad lib.

D.S. al 🏵 poi al Coda

CODA   rall.

(Ped.)

2. St. Louis Blues

Words and music by W.C. Handy

3. That Lovin' Rag

Victor H. Smalley & Bernard Adler

* Small notes ad lib.

4. Jelly Roll Blues

Ferd (Jelly Roll) Morton

Moderate blues tempo ♩ = 144

* small notes ad lib.

5. Red Peppers

(A two-step)

Imogene Giles

6. Royal Garden Blues

Spencer Williams
& Clarence Williams.
Arranged by Billy Amstell.

7. The Lily Rag

Chas. Thompson

* Small notes ad lib.

Ped.